Watching
Orangutans
in Asia

Deborah Underwood

Heinemann Library
Chicago, Illinois

Customer Service   888-454-2279
Visit our website at www.heinemannlibrary.com

Designed by Ron Kamen and edesign
Illustrations by Martin Sanders
Printed and bound in China by South China Printing Company Limited

10 09 08 07 06
10 9 8 7 6 5 4 3 2 1

Library of Congress Cataloging-in-Publication Data
Underwood, Deborah.
  Watching orangutans in Asia / Deborah Underwood.
      p. cm. -- (Wild world)
  Includes bibliographical references. ISBN 1-4034-7231-9 (hardback : alk. paper) -- ISBN 1-4034-7244-0 (pbk. : alk. paper)
  1. Orangutan--Juvenile literature. I. Title. II. Series: Wild world (Chicago, Ill.)
  QL737.P96U57 2006
  599.88'3--dc22
                                        2005023643
Acknowledgments
The author and publisher are grateful to the following for permission to reproduce copyright material: Ardea pp. **5**
(Adrian Warren), **7** (Jean Paul Ferrero), **17** (M. Watson), **20** (Masahiro Iijima); Corbis p. **27**; FLPA pp. **4** (Konrad
Wthe/Minden Pictures), **11** (Mark Newman), **24** (Frans Lanting/Minden Pictures); Nature Picture Library pp. **10** (Anup
Shah), **12** (Anup Shah), **14** (Anup Shah), **15** (Anup Shah), **16** (Anup Shah), **18** (Ingo Arndt), **19** (Anup Shah), **23** (Anup
Shah), **25** (Anup Shah), **26** (Mark Linfield); NPHA pp. **8**, **9** (Nick Garbutt), **22**; Steve Bloom p. **21**; Still Images p. **13**.
Cover photograph of a mother orangutan and baby reproduced with permission of Nature Picture Library (Anup Shah).

The publishers would like to thank Michael Bright of the BBC Natural History Unit for his assistance in the preparation of
this book. Every effort has been made to contact copyright holders of any material reproduced in this book. Any
omissions will be rectified in subsequent printings if notice is given to the publisher. The paper used to print this book
comes from sustainable resources.publication.

Some words are shown in bold, **like this**. You can find out
what they mean by looking in the glossary.

Contents

Meet the Orangutans

This is Asia, the home of orangutans. Long ago, people gave these apes the name *orang hutan*. These words mean "person of the forest."

▶▶ *It is easy to see why some people once thought orangutans were human.*

Orangutans belong to the **great ape** family. Like all great apes, they are very smart. Chimpanzees and gorillas are also great apes.

Orangutans are related to gorillas like this one.

5

Island Homes

Borneo and Sumatra are large **islands** near the **continent** of Asia. Long ago, orangutans lived all over Southeast Asia. Now they only live here.

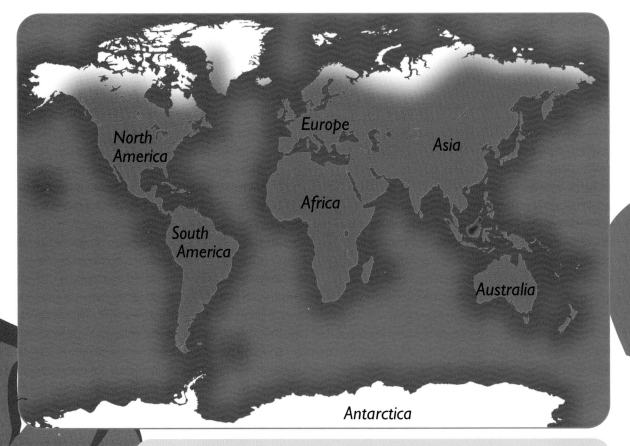

North America

Europe

Asia

Africa

South America

Australia

Antarctica

Key   ● *This color shows where orangutans live in Asia.*

The islands are near the **equator**. The weather here is warm and damp. The Sun shines for twelve hours each day. Heavy rains fall for part of the year.

Borneo and Sumatra have only two seasons: rainy and dry.

Rain Forests

Orangutans live in **rain forests**. Trees reach up to the sky. Their thick leaves block the Sun's rays. Very little light reaches the forest floor.

▶▶ *Rain forests give orangutans many kinds of food to eat.*

Orangutans share the rain forest with many plants and animals.

The rain forest is home to thousands of kinds of animals. Some live on the forest floor. Others live high in the trees.

There's an Orangutan!

Orangutans often hang from the trees.
Their long red hair helps them blend into
the shadows.

▶▶ *Orangutans are shorter*
than most humans, but
much stronger.

long arms

toes for gripping

red hair

Orangutans have long arms, long hands, and long feet. They can grasp branches with their toes. **Males** are more than twice as big as **females**.

◀◀ *Full-grown males have cheek pads.*

On the Move

Orangutans pull themselves from tree to tree. They are heavy, so they move carefully. They make sure each branch can hold their weight.

▼ *Baby orangutans hold on tight as they are carried through the trees.*

▲ *Orangutans can use their hands and feet to grab branches.*

Sometimes an orangutan cannot reach the next tree. It rocks back and forth. This makes the tree bend. When it bends enough, the orangutan can grab the next tree.

Alone in the Trees

Orangutans spend nearly all their time in the trees. Young orangutans live with their mothers. Adult **males** almost always live alone.

▲ *Orangutans do not live in groups like other **great apes**.*

A male makes a long, noisy call. The sound warns other males to keep away. It may also help **females** find a **mate** in the thick forest.

A male's long call can be heard from far away.

Orangutan Babies

After she found a **mate**, one of the **females** had a baby. Baby orangutans are helpless. Their mothers feed them, carry them, and protect them.

▶▶ *Female orangutans have a baby about every eight years.*

▲ *Babies are carried on their mothers' backs.*

The young orangutan will stay with its mother for years. She will teach it how to find foods that are safe to eat.

Finding Food

Orangutans eat many different foods. They like fruit best. They also eat bark, leaves, flowers, and **insects**. They spend most of the day looking for food.

▼ *When they can't find fruit, orangutans eat other plants or insects.*

Different trees make fruit at different times. Orangutans remember when the best trees will have fruit. They make sure to visit these trees when the fruit is **ripe**.

▼ *Orangutans will go out of their way to visit a favorite fruit tree.*

How Orangutans Eat

Some forest foods can be tricky to eat. Sharp points protect the fruit of the **durian** tree. An orangutan must work hard to get at its food.

▶▶ *Durians smell awful, but orangutans love the sweet taste.*

A mother orangutan prepares her meal. She throws away seeds and **husks**. Her child watches carefully. It learns which parts of each food are good to eat.

▲ *Sometimes a young orangutan takes food from its mother's mouth.*

Sleeping Nests

As it gets dark, orangutans begin to make nests to sleep in. They make new nests from tree branches each evening.

▲ *Orangutans sometimes make nests for naps during the day.*

When the nests are ready, the orangutans settle in for the night. Young orangutans share nests with their mothers.

▼ *Sharing nests with their mothers keeps young orangutans safe.*

23

Rainy Season

The rainy season begins late in the year. Sheets of rain pour from the sky. Rivers swell. Fewer fruits can be found. Orangutans must eat more bark and leaves.

⩔ *Heavy rain keeps the **rain forest** green.*

24

Most orangutans do not like to get wet. They make umbrellas out of leaves. They hold the leaves over their heads to keep the water off.

Leaves help orangutans stay dry when it rains.

Under Attack

Tigers may kill some orangutans. But human hunters are a much bigger problem. Hunters kill orangutan mothers so their babies can be sold as pets.

▲ *Tigers on Sumatra may hunt orangutans.*

Each year the **rain forest** gets smaller. People cut down its trees to get wood. But many others are working hard to save the orangutans' forest home.

If we cut down the rain forests, orangutans will have nowhere to live.

Tracker's Guide

When you want to watch animals in the wild, you need to find them first. You can look for clues they leave behind.

▶▶ *If you listen carefully, you might hear an orangutan moving through the trees.*

◄◄ A sleeping nest high in a tree means that an orangutan has been here!

▲ Orangutans can be messy eaters. You might find some dropped food.

Glossary

continent the world is split into seven large areas of land called continents. Each continent is divided into different countries.

durian smelly fruit with a hard, thorny shell

equator the pretend line that goes around the center of the globe

female animal that can become a mother when it grows up. Women and girls are female people.

great ape one of a group of animals that includes orangutans, chimpanzees, and gorillas

husk dry outer part of some fruits and seeds

insect tiny creature with six legs

island area of land with water all around it

male animal that can become a father when it grows up. Men and boys are male people.

mate when male and female animals produce young

rain forest place where many trees and plants grow close together and where lots of rain falls

ripe ready to eat

Find Out More

Books

Dennard, Deborah. *Orangutans*. Chanhassen, Minn.: NorthWord Press, 2003.

Foster, Leila. *Asia*. Chicago: Heinemann Library, 2001.

Ganeri, Anita. *Animal Life Cycles*. Chicago: Heinemann Library, 2005.

Kendell, Patricia. *Orangutans*. Chicago: Raintree, 2004.

Murray, Julia. *Orangutans*. Minneapolis, Minn.: ABDO Publishing Company, 2005.

Whitehouse, Patricia. *Hiding in a Rain Forest*. Chicago: Heinemann Library, 2003.

An older reader can help you with these books:

Martin, Patricia A. Fink. *Orangutans*. New York: Children's Press, 2000.

Pyers, Greg. *Why Am I a Mammal?* Chicago: Raintree, 2005.

Index